THE MICROSTRUCTURE OF CELLS

Labels on figure: fragments of endoplasmic reticulum; nucleus; part of new cell wall forming between newly formed cells; mitochondria; cell wall

FIG. 1.1. A group of cells from root tip of maize, passing through the junction of the root tip and root proper. Each cell contains a nucleus, groups of mitochondria and fragments of endoplasmic reticulum. No vacuoles have formed. In the left of the photograph cell walls in early stages of formation can be seen, but around most of the cells very thick walls can be seen. *Magnification × 2625.*

Courtesy of Dr B. E. Juniper

STEPHEN W. HURRY

The Microstructure of Cells

AN INTRODUCTION FOR SIXTH FORMS

With a foreword by P. B. MEDAWAR CBE FRS

JOHN MURRAY ALBEMARLE STREET LONDON

Acknowledgments

I should like to offer my thanks to the many people who have helped me in writing this book. In particular I am very grateful to Dr P. B. Medawar CBE FRS, Professor A. R. Ubbelohde CBE FRS and Miss Georgina Greene for their constant encouragement, constructive criticism and good advice. To Mr A. D. Greenwood, Dr B. E. Juniper, Dr G. F. Elliott and Mr D. G. Mackean I am grateful for their criticisms and helpful suggestions after they had read the manuscript. For permission to reproduce illustrations I have to thank the large number of people who are individually acknowledged in the legends, and I also acknowledge with pleasure the courtesy of numerous publishers who have permitted me to reproduce figures from books and periodicals. Professor R. D. Preston FRS, Dr H. E. Huxley FRS, Dr W. Bernhard, Mr A. D. Greenwood, Dr B. E. Juniper, Mrs C. F. Schoenburg, Dr D. S. Smith, and Dr A. V. Grimstone, have given me illustrations previously unpublished and I am particularly in their debt for their kindness.

S. W. HURRY

NOTES ON REFERENCES

To avoid repetition, the following works are referred to in the credit lines by title only:

The Cell, 2nd edn, ed. by Brachet, E. and Mirsky, H. E. (Academic Press, New York/London, 1961)

A Textbook of Histology, 8th edn, Bloom, W. and Fawcett, D. W. (W. B. Saunders Co., Philadelphia, 1962)

Fourth International Conference on Electron Microscopy (Springer-Verlag, Berlin/Göttingen/Heidelberg, 1960)

Fifth International Conference on Electron Microscopy. Vol. 2 (Academic Press, New York/London, 1962)

Printed in Great Britain by
William Clowes and Sons Ltd, London and Beccles
and published by John Murray (Publishers) Ltd
50 Albemarle Street, London W.1

Foreword

This book is one of the outward signs of a quiet revolution which over the past ten or fifteen years has transformed our whole conception of the 'physical basis of life'.

Many theories of the structure of protoplasm were propounded in the early days of critical microscopy: an 'alveolar' theory for one, and a 'reticular' theory for another. In the first few years of this century Sir William Hardy and others showed that the alveolar and reticular appearances of protoplasm under the microscope were illusory, at least in the sense that they depended on the particular methods used to 'fix' cells in preparing them for microscopic examination. With the growth of colloid chemistry (at one time believed to be a branch of chemistry in its own right with laws of colloidal behaviour peculiar to itself) the idea gained ground that protoplasm, optically homogeneous under the microscope, was quite structureless in any ordinary anatomical sense. Nothing challenged the idea of protoplasm as a sort of pervasive biological ether or primordial slime, a fragile and highly complex colloidal system in which the properties of life resided. I believe that Frederick Gowland Hopkins had this idea in mind when in an address to the British Association in 1913 he declared that the life of the cell was 'the expression of a particular dynamic equilibrium in a polyphasic system'.

By the early 1930's enough had been learnt of cellular metabolism to make it quite sure that, no matter to what degree of complexity it might be elaborated, the colloidal picture of cellular organization was simply not good enough. What could be the physical basis of the orderliness of cellular metabolism—of the fact that each episode in a complex metabolic sequence happened in the right order and in the right place? It seemed natural to look for a structural basis, and led by R. A. Peters people began to think in terms of a 'cytoskeleton'. But then how was the existence of a cytoskeleton to be reconciled with the fact that the eggs of certain echinoderms could resume normal development after their contents had been stratified into neat layers in the ultracentrifuge?

This was an awkward period in the development of cellular biology. It was quite clear that there was really no such thing as 'protoplasm', and anyone who claimed to be studying the nature and properties of protoplasm would have been thought facetious or slightly mad. But though protoplasm had been deposed (and with it the whole colloidal conception of cellular organization) it had no heir.

The interregnum lasted fifteen or twenty years. The conception that has superseded the idea of protoplasm can literally be seen in the pages of Mr Stephen Hurry's present book. A cell is a highly heterogeneous system of *structures* in an almost crudely anatomical sense. Cells contain tubes and sheets and even micro-organs—real anatomical structures in the sense that they have definite shapes and look as if only their size prevented our picking them up and handling them. In short, the orderliness of the working of a cell is a solid or crystalline orderliness (the so-called amorphous solids, said Schrodinger, are either not amorphous or not solid). There is, moreover, no dividing line between the chemists' structures and the anatomists'. The large molecules of proteins and nucleic acids have a 'structure' in a sense intelligible to anatomists, and small anatomical objects like chromosomes could be described as molecules in a sense intelligible to chemists.

The revolution I have described started with X-ray crystallography—it was a tremendous thing when, thirty-odd years ago, Astbury's X-ray diffraction photomicrographs of feathers and hairs revealed a crystalline regularity of structure—and the biochemists who first showed that cellular particles would respire had a good deal to do with it; but mainly, of course, it has been the work of electron microscopy, and Mr Hurry's admirably chosen illustrations and apt text give a pretty good idea of its range and power. One may look in vain through these pages for 'protoplasm': structure is all one will find; and one can see too how far cellular biology is on the way to becoming 'molecular biology', the state of knowledge in which a biological performance can be *explicitly* related to molecular structure. It is most satisfactory that the newer knowledge of cellular organization should now so quickly be made available to advanced students of biology in schools.

P. B. MEDAWAR

Contents

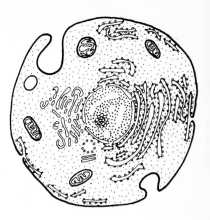

1 · The Cell

Judged solely on the basis of the number of cell types in a multicellular body, the cell is a highly adaptable structure. For cells exist in a great variety of forms and fulfil a great variety of functions; nevertheless it is possible to discern a basic common pattern.

Around the outside of the cell is a thin membrane, the plasma membrane. In plant cells generally, but not in animal cells, a rigid non-living cell wall lies outside the plasma mem-

brane (Fig. 1.1). Inside the plasma membrane is the cytoplasm of the cell. The cytoplasm is differentiated into several kinds of structure, and these are often referred to as subcellular organelles. These include mitochondria, centrioles, endoplasmic reticulum, the Golgi apparatus and ribosomes (Figs. 1.2 and 1.3). As well as these organelles the cytoplasm may contain granules and crystals of non-living material, fluid-filled vacuoles, droplets of oil and pigments. The nucleus, a very

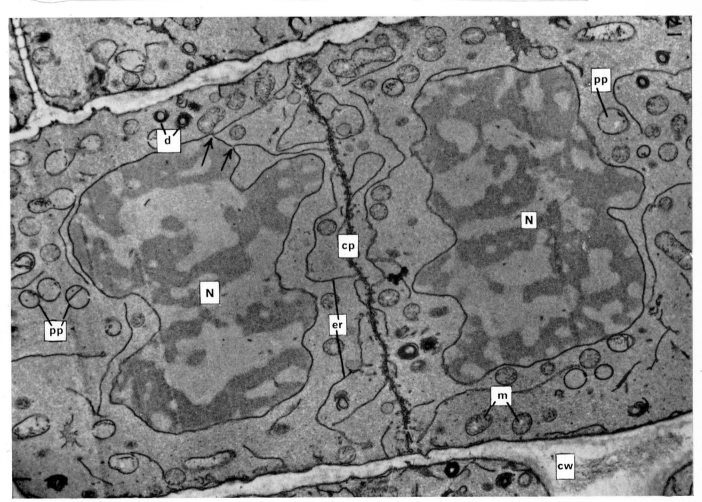

FIG. 1.2. Cells from onion root tip just after mitosis has taken place. The two nuclei [N] have re-formed and are surrounded by nuclear envelopes, but in the upper cell the envelope is continuous with endoplasmic reticulum [er] (arrowed). The cytoplasm of the two cells is incompletely divided by the cell plate on which the cell wall [cw] will later be deposited. In the cytoplasm of both cells mitochondria (m) and proplastids (pp) can be seen, while at (d) portions of the Golgi apparatus are visible. The two daughter cells are surrounded by a thick cell wall. *Magnification × 7000.*

From Porter K., in The Cell

7

highly specialised membrane-bounded body, often occurs in the centre of the cell.

The arrangement of the subcellular components inside the cell varies widely from cell type to cell type and during the life history of a single type of cell. Very often the endoplasmic reti-culum occupies the greater part of the cytoplasm. Usually the centrioles, Golgi apparatus and mitochondria lie freely be-tween the folds of this reticulum. The matrix in which they lie appears to be homogeneous although in some cells it contains very fine fibres (see Fig. 5.1).

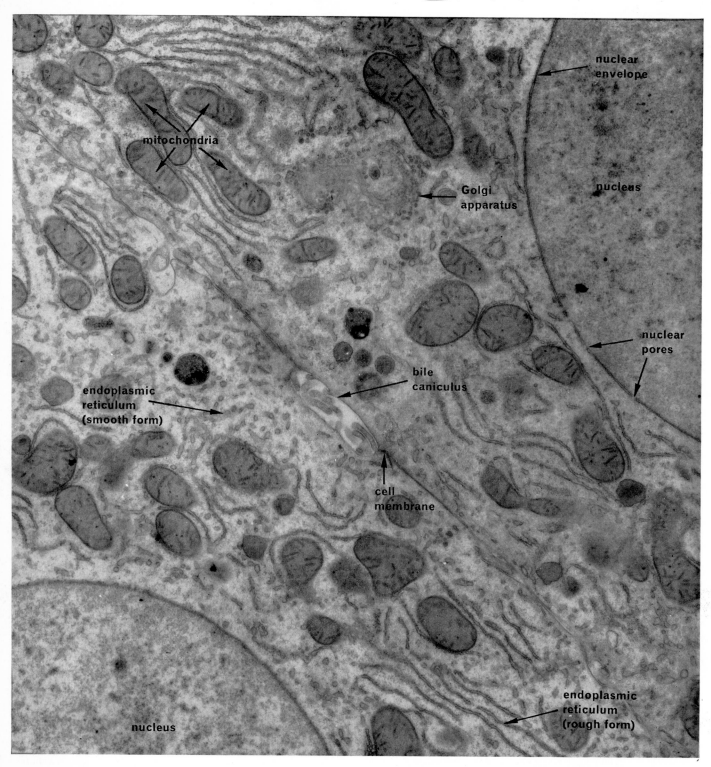

FIG. 1.3. A portion of two cells from rat liver. As in the plant cell of Fig. 1.1 mitochondria and endo-plasmic reticulum are clearly visible, and portions of the nucleus of each cell can also be seen. There is no cell wall between the two cells. In many places the endoplasmic reticulum has granules on it, but the agranular form of endoplasmic reticulum can also be seen in the lower cell. The double layer of nuclear membrane can be seen round the nucleus on the right and several pores in the membrane can be made out. A prominent feature of the upper cell is the Golgi apparatus. *Magnification* × *16,300.*

From Porter K., in The Cell

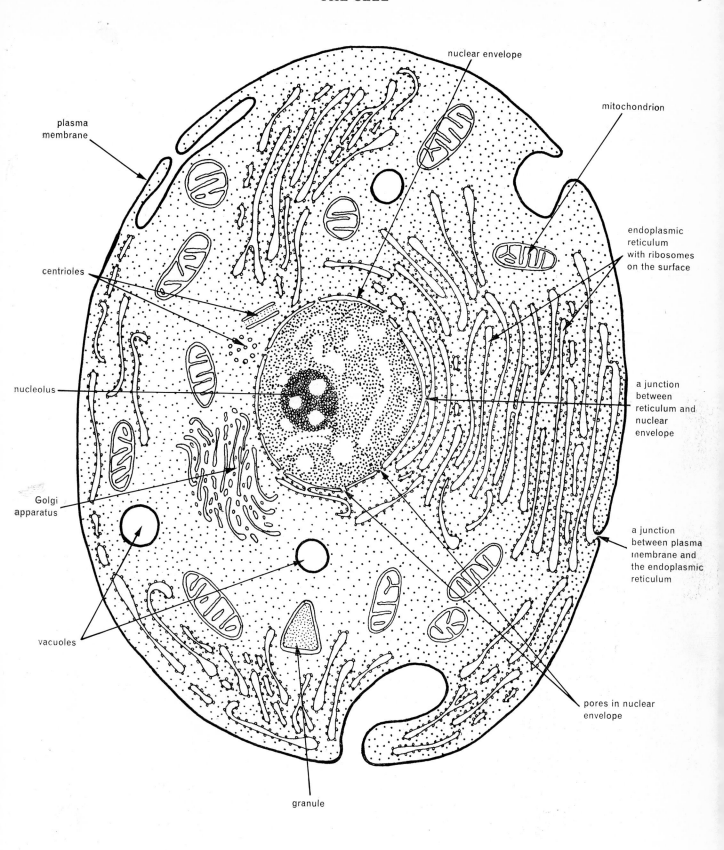

plasma membrane

centrioles

nucleolus

Golgi apparatus

vacuoles

nuclear envelope

mitochondrion

endoplasmic reticulum with ribosomes on the surface

a junction between reticulum and nuclear envelope

a junction between plasma membrane and the endoplasmic reticulum

pores in nuclear envelope

granule

FIG. 1.4. Diagrammatic generalised cell to show the relationships between the various components of the cell.

2 · The Cell Wall

It is a characteristic of plants that their cells are surrounded by a non-living layer of material, the cell wall (Fig. 2.1). Animal cells are usually naked except for the plasma membrane. The cell wall is produced by the cell itself; the first signs of it appear during the final stages of cell division, after the nucleus has divided but before the cytoplasm has separated. In the cytoplasm fine droplets fuse to form a thin layer across the cell, which is believed to correspond to the middle lamella. Later, layers of cellulose are deposited on the middle lamella, forming in turn the primary, secondary and in some cases even a tertiary cell wall.

Cellulose, which forms the framework of the cell wall, is laid down in bundles of parallel macrofibrils. The macrofibrils are

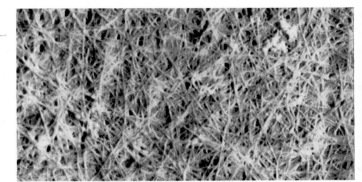

FIG. 2.2. Surface view of primary cell wall of *Valonia*. The cellulose microfibrils run in all directions and form a complex structure. *Magnification × 16,500.*

From Mühlethaler K., *in* The Cell

in a thin layer of scattered macrofibrils; this is the primary cell wall (Fig. 2.2).

On the primary wall the secondary wall is deposited. This may be a thick wall with up to three layers in it. In contrast to the scattered macrofibrils of the primary wall, the macrofibrils of the secondary wall are close-packed in parallel array (Fig. 2.3). Each layer of macrofibrils, however, is laid down in a different direction, often at about 120° to the previous layer (Fig. 2.4).

The tertiary wall, which is present in some plants, is a thin, homogeneous, structureless layer.

Xylem cells are strengthened by thick bands of cellulose laid down as rings, helices, or as nets on the primary wall. The lignification which occurs in these cells is confined to the bands.

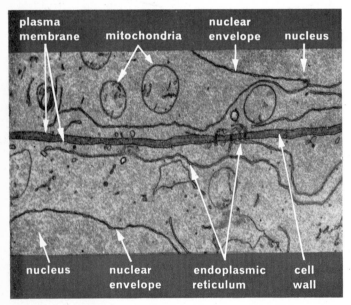

FIG. 2.1. A part of two cells from maize root cap, showing the cell wall between the two cells. Portion of the nucleus, nuclear envelope, endoplasmic reticulum and mitochondria can be seen in the cytoplasm of both cells. The plasma membrane of both cells is very close to the wall between the cells but is visible as a thin dark line. *Magnification × 10,600.*

Courtesy of Dr B. E. Juniper

in turn made up of bundles of about 400 microfibrils. Each microfibril has a diameter of 100–250 Å and may be several microns long, being made up of about 2000 cellulose molecules. The spaces between the bundles of macrofibrils are filled with encrusting substances, e.g. pectin and hemicellulose.

The deposition of the cellulose of the primary wall starts at the middle lamella and proceeds inwards: cellulose is laid down

FIG. 2.3. Surface view of secondary cell wall of *Valonia*. The cellulose macrofibrils are arranged in sheets of parallel fibrils, each sheet orientated across the sheet below. *Magnification × 16,500.*

From Mühlethaler K., *in* The Cell

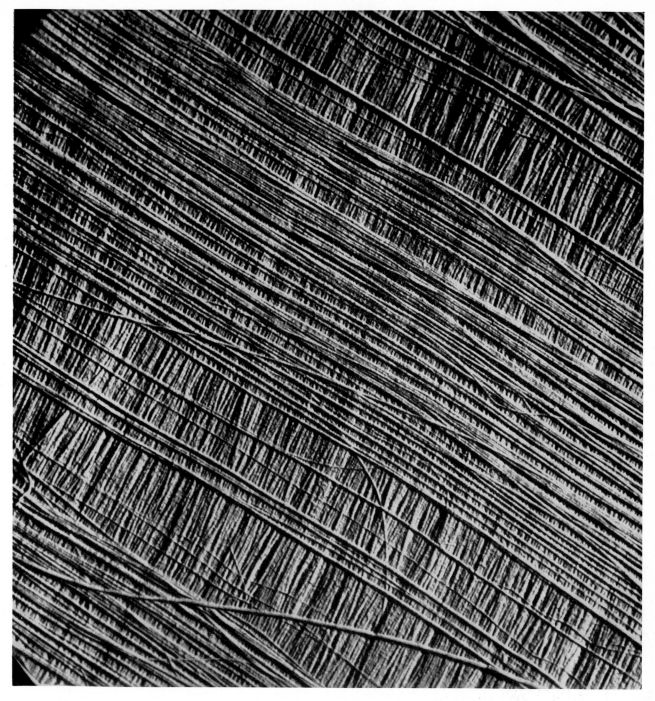

FIG. 2.4. Surface view of cell wall of *Chaetomorpha*. The very regular arrangement of the macrofibrils is clearly seen on this photograph. *Magnification × 30,000.*

Courtesy of Professor R. D. Preston

3 · The Cell Membrane

The living cell is never in equilibrium with its environment, for water and dissolved materials are continuously being exchanged between the cell and its surroundings. The control of these processes depends to a great extent on the membrane bounding the cell (Fig. 3.1). Amongst the many hypotheses on the nature of the membrane that have been proposed, that of Danielli and Davson has been widely accepted. They visualised the cell membrane as a double layer of lipid material coated with a layer of protein on each side. (It is now generally agreed that there is a carbohydrate component as well.) They estimated the thickness of the membrane at about 80 Å.

Analysis of x-ray diffraction patterns and measurement of electron micrographs have confirmed the Danielli–Davson hypothesis: they indicate that there are two layers of material each about 25–40 Å wide with a band between them of about 20–40 Å, giving a total minimum width of about 70 Å. This is now known as the unit membrane (Fig. 3.2). Membranes of these dimensions with chemical properties very similar to those predicted for them have been studied in a wide variety of animal and plant cells. In addition the double membranes (consisting of two unit-membranes) of the Golgi apparatus, mitochondria and the endoplasmic reticulum and nucleus show a similar structure. This can be explained by the hypothesis that these internal membranes were derived from the cell membrane, by folding inwards from the surface of the cell.

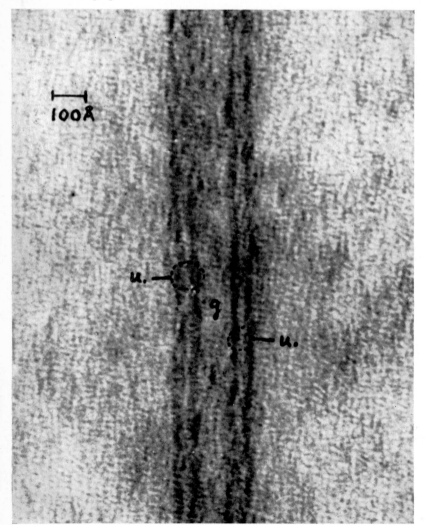

FIG. 3.1 (*opposite*). Cell membrane of a red blood cell. The membrane can be seen to possess a three-layered structure. Such a membrane is called a unit membrane. *Magnification × 360,000.*

From Robertson J. D., *in* Sci. Amer., *206:4, April 1962*

FIG. 3.2 (*left*). A pair of unit membranes from myelin sheath of sciatic nerve of mouse. Each membrane (marked u) can be seen to be made up of three layers. Separating the membranes is a layer of myelin (g).

From Robertson J. D., *in* Biochem. Soc. Symp. *16:3, 1959*

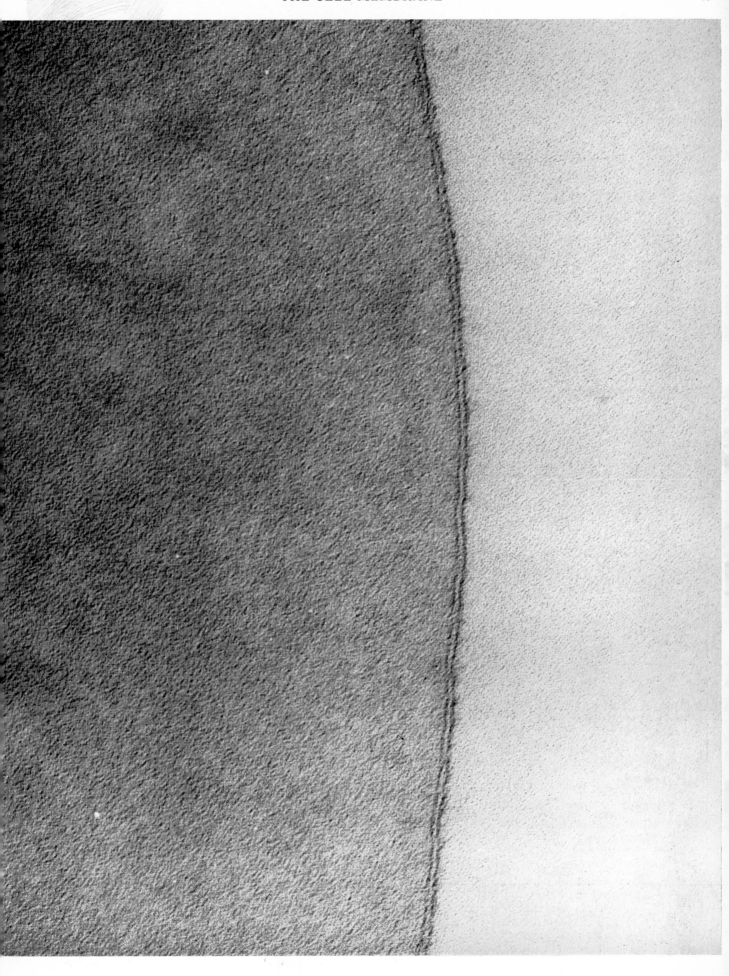

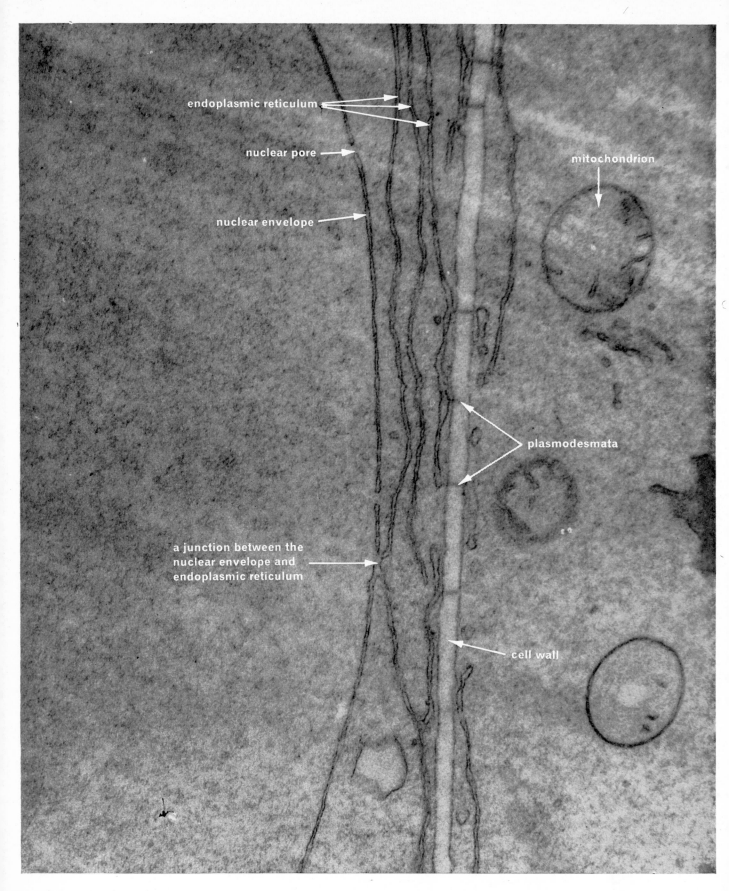

endoplasmic reticulum

nuclear pore

nuclear envelope

mitochondrion

plasmodesmata

a junction between the
nuclear envelope and
endoplasmic reticulum

cell wall

FIG. 4.1. Part of two cells from maize root. The endoplasmic reticulum can be very clearly seen to be made of two membranes with a space between them. A junction between the nuclear envelope and the endoplasmic reticulum is visible and two nuclear pores can also be seen. The endoplasmic reticulum does not appear to be granular in this photograph. Running through the cell wall between the two cells are plasmodesmata; these seem to connect the endoplasmic reticulum of the two cells. In the cell on the right three mitochondria are visible. *Magnification × 30,000.*

From Whaley W. G., Mollenhauer H. H., and Kephart J., in Biophys. Biochem. Cytol. *5:3, 1959*

4 · The Endoplasmic Reticulum

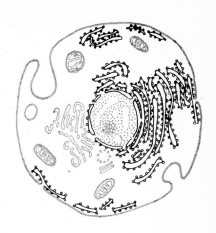

The cytoplasm of cells is now thought to consist of a matrix, called hyaloplasm, in which are embedded ribosomes and very fine fibrils (100 Å diameter) of several kinds, and various structures surrounded by membranes, including the Golgi apparatus and the endoplasmic reticulum. In the cells of all highly developed animals and plants, except the mammalian erythrocyte, bacteria and blue-green algae, the reticulum is differentiated into a nuclear envelope and often continuous with it is a cytoplasmic reticulum (Fig. 4.1). The cytoplasmic portion of the membrane system is often called the endoplasmic reticulum. This reticulum consists of a continuous and morphologically highly variable system of flattened sacs and tubules separated from the matrix by a membrane 40 Å thick. Two forms of this membrane have been described. In one form the surface of the membrane in contact with the cytoplasm is heavily coated with ribosomal particles (Fig. 4.2). This type of

membrane has been seen in both animal and plant cells; it is abundant in growing cells and in cells in which protein synthesis is occurring, e.g. acinar cells of the pancreas, and is characteristically present as flat fluid-filled vesicles. In meristematic cells of plants there is, however, only a small amount of this kind of membrane.

The second type of cytoplasmic membrane which has so far

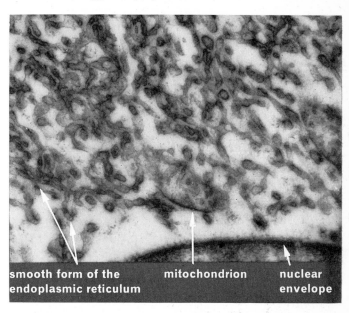

FIG. 4.3. Part of cell from interstitial tissue of opossum testis. The endoplasmic reticulum in this cell has no ribosomal granules and is called the smooth or agranular form of the e.r. (cf. Fig. 4.2). The tubular cisternae branch and rejoin to form a complex network. *Magnification × 33,000.*

From Christensen A. K. and Fawcett D. W.,
in J. Biophy. Biochem. Cytol. *9, 1961*

not been found in plant cells is smooth on both surfaces and is present in tubes of diameter 500–1000 Å, making a complex lattice in the cell (Fig. 4.3). The smooth form occurs in cells secreting steroids.

Both forms of membrane may be present in a single cell, e.g. striated muscle cells. The origin, the fate and behaviour of the endoplasmic reticulum during cell division are uncertain. Various functions have been suggested for the endoplasmic reticulum, including protein synthesis, glycogen storage, steroid synthesis, intra-cellular transport and intra-cellular impulse conduction in striated muscle cells.

The ribosomal particles on the rough form of the endoplasmic reticulum are thought to be the site of protein synthesis in

FIG. 4.2. The Nissl substance from Purkinje cells of the rat. Four parallel sheets of the endoplasmic reticulum with many granules on their surface can be seen here in section. The granules are ribosomes and occur free in the cytoplasm as well as on the endoplasmic reticulum membranes. Notice that no granules occur in the cavity of the endoplasmic reticulum cistenae. *Magnification × 67,000.*

Photograph by S. L. Palay, in A Textbook of Histology

the cell. It is at the ribosomes that the amino acids which make up the proteins are assembled and joined together, but the parts played in the process by the ribosomes of the cytoplasm and the ribosomes on the reticulum respectively are not understood. Chemically, ribosomes are very rich in ribonucleic acid (RNA) and proteins; part of this RNA is derived from the nucleus and part from the matrix. Genetic information carried in the nucleus is transcribed into specific proteins outside the nucleus, the nuclear RNA of the ribosomes acting as a messenger from the nucleus.

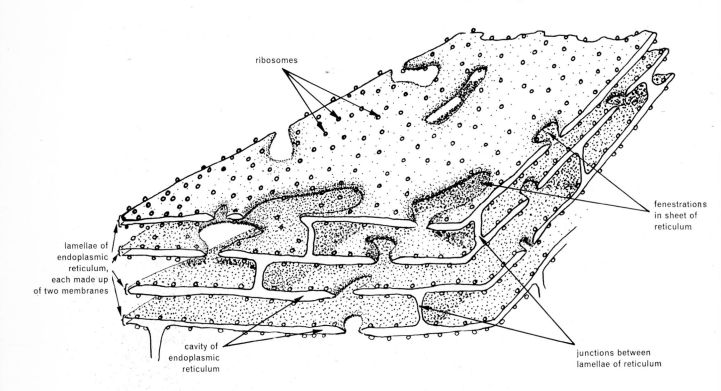

FIG. 4.4. Stereogram to show general structure of granular endoplasmic reticulum, made up of parallel lamellae which are joined to adjacent lamellae and are penetrated by large fenestrations.

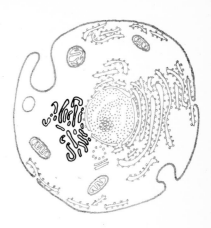

5 · The Golgi Apparatus

The Golgi apparatus, like the endoplasmic reticulum, is a system of flattened sacs at the margins of large vacuoles, with clusters of small vacuoles from the periphery of the flattened sacs (Fig. 5.1). Unlike the endoplasmic reticulum the membranes of the Golgi apparatus are smooth and not crusted with ribosomes (Fig. 5.2). The position and size of the Golgi apparatus vary from one cell type to another. It is well developed in secretory cells and neurones, but small in muscle cells. It may be found around the nucleus, as in neurones, or between the nucleus and the periphery of the cell. The sacs and vacuoles are fluid-filled, but neither the fluid contents nor the membranes themselves have enzymes associated with them. The role of the apparatus in cells in which it occurs is not known with any certainty at the moment; it may be involved in storage and possibly modification of lipids in some cell types. A secretory function has been suggested for the Golgi

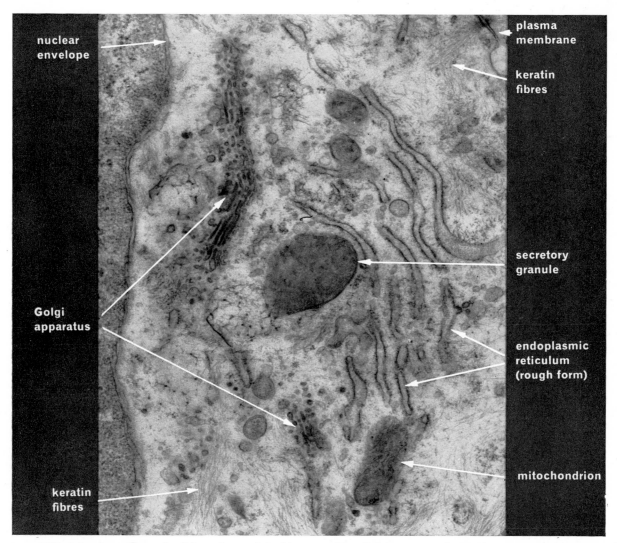

FIG. 5.1. An epidermal cell from larva of Amblystoma. The Golgi apparatus is seen here as a prominent mass of flattened tubules arranged roughly parallel with each other and with swollen ends. *Magnification × 21,200.*

From Porter K., in The Cell

apparatus in some animal cells, but not definitely confirmed. It may well be the case that the function of the Golgi apparatus varies during the life of a cell. In plant cells the Golgi apparatus is usually much less extensive than is the case in animal cells, although there are exceptions to this, e.g. peripheral cells of the root cap in plants.

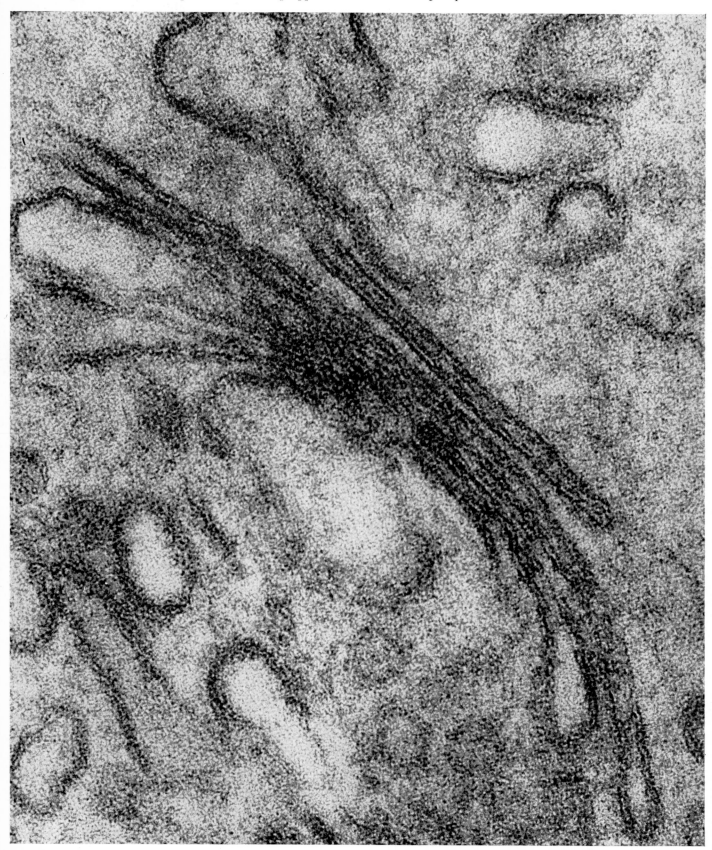

FIG. 5.2.   The Golgi apparatus can be seen here to be made up of flattened sacs, the membrane boundaries of which show a clear triple layer structure, i.e. each is a unit membrane. *Magnification × 360,000.*

From Robertson J. D., in Sci. Amer., 206:4, April 1962

6 · Mitochondria

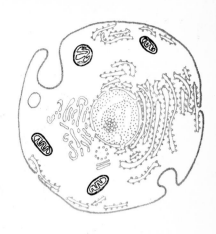

Mitochondria are usually from 0·5 to 1μ in diameter and vary in length up to 400μ. They consist of 65–70% protein, 25–30% lipids and 0·5% RNA. Very large numbers of mitochondria may be present in a cell (500,000 in Chaos, 500–1400 in rat liver cells). While their shape and number are variable, their general structure appears to be similar in all cells so far examined. Each consists of a double-walled, rod-like structure with rounded ends and sides (Fig. 6.1). The outer membrane is smooth and essentially similar in all cells that have so far been adequately studied. The inner membrane has a variable structure and is produced into a series of interdigitating shelves or cristae which may be longitudinally or transversely orientated, branched or tubular (Figs. 6.2, 6.3 and 6.4). This arrangement greatly increases the surface area inside the mitochondria. It is thought that either in the fluid-filled matrix between the cristae, or more likely attached to the surface of the cristae, are the enzymes catalysing the Krebs cycle and fatty acid oxidation. Small granules about the same size as ribosomes have been found on the inner faces of cristae, and it is suggested that these are the actual sites of energy transfer (Fig. 6.8). The mitochondria are organelles which transfer the chemical energy of the metabolites of the cell into the cell's energy-using systems.

Mitochondria sometimes occupy fixed positions in the cell, as in insect striated muscle cells where they are arranged in rings around the myofibrils, and in kidney tubule cells where they are anchored to the cell membrane (Figs. 6.5 and 6.6). In other cells the mitochondria are swept around the cell in the protoplasmic streaming.

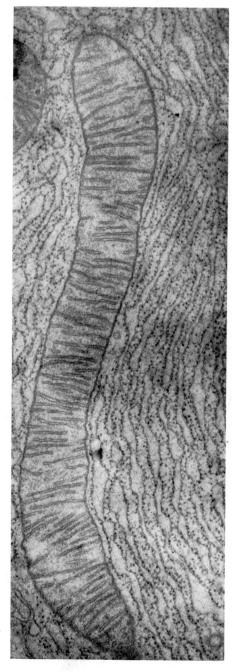

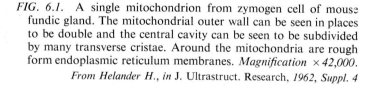

FIG. 6.1. A single mitochondrion from zymogen cell of mouse fundic gland. The mitochondrial outer wall can be seen in places to be double and the central cavity can be seen to be subdivided by many transverse cristae. Around the mitochondria are rough form endoplasmic reticulum membranes. *Magnification* ×42,000.

From Helander H., in J. Ultrastruct. Research, *1962, Suppl. 4*

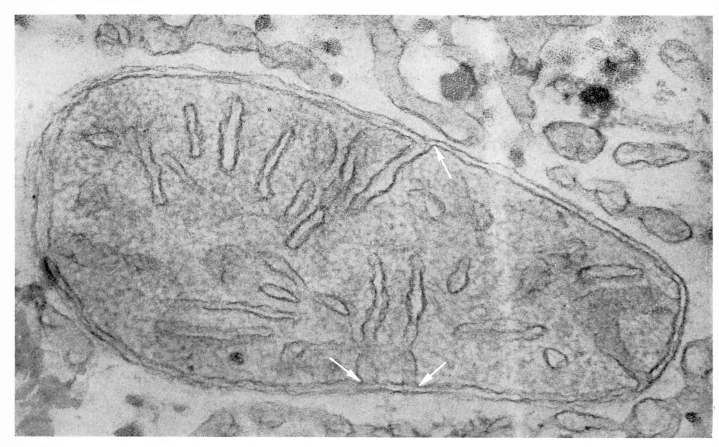

FIG. 6.2.   A single mitochondrion from rat liver cell. The junctions between the transverse cristae and the inner wall (arrowed) and the membrane forming the outer wall can very clearly be seen. *Magnification × 235,000.*

Photography by M. L. Watson (article by A. Lehninger), in Sci. Amer., 202:5, May, 1960. Professor Watson's work performed partly under contract with the United States Atomic Energy Commission at the University of Rochester and partly under Research Grant CY-3589 from the National Institutes of Health, United States Public Health Service.

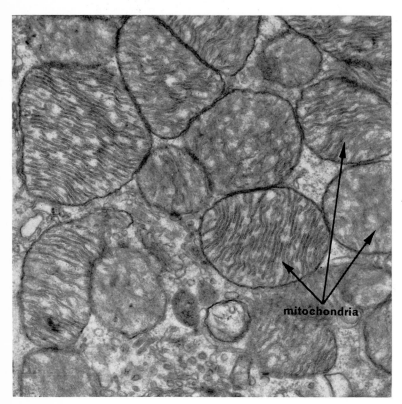

FIG. 6.3.   Mitochondria in cardiac muscle of the mouse. The cristae are arranged very close together in these mitochondria.

Courtesy of Dr D. S. Smith

FIG. 6.4. Mitochondria from flight muscle of *Pieris*. The section is cut along the length of the mitochondria and shows a very closely packed array of cristae. *Magnification × 42,000.*

Courtesy of Dr D. S. Smith

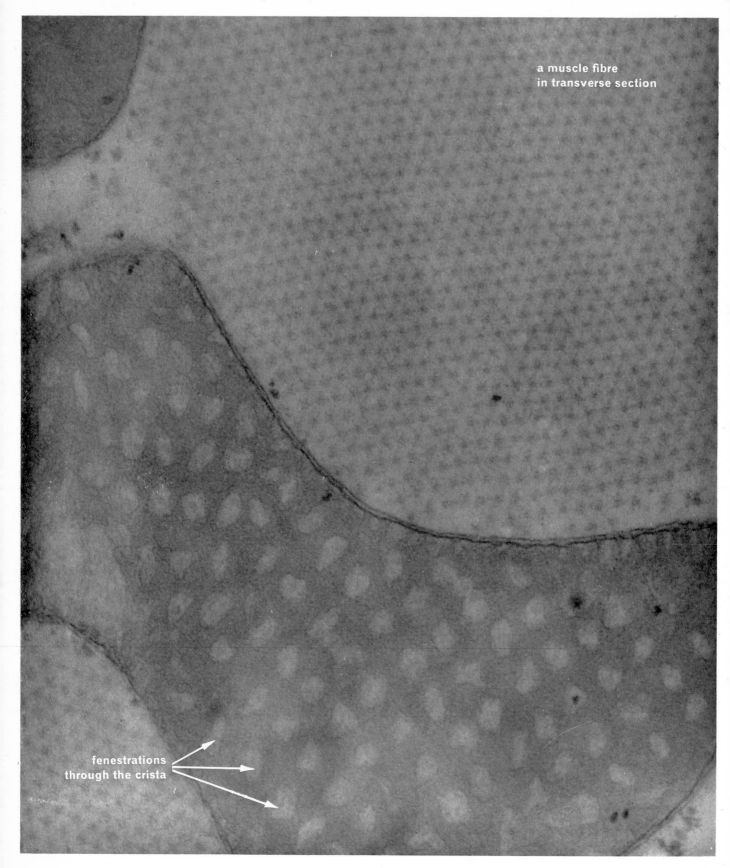

a muscle fibre
in transverse section

fenestrations
through the crista

FIG. 6.5.   Mitochondria from flight muscle of *Pieris*. The section is at right angles to the plane of Fig. 6.4 and
is parallel to the direction of the cristae. The cristae are fenestrated. These fenestrations appear as gaps in
the cristae in Fig. 6.4, each gap aligned behind a corresponding gap in preceding cristae. *Magnification
× 188,000 (approx).*

Courtesy of Dr D. S. Smith

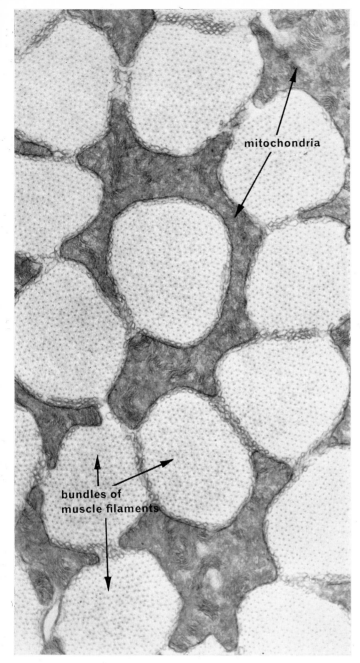

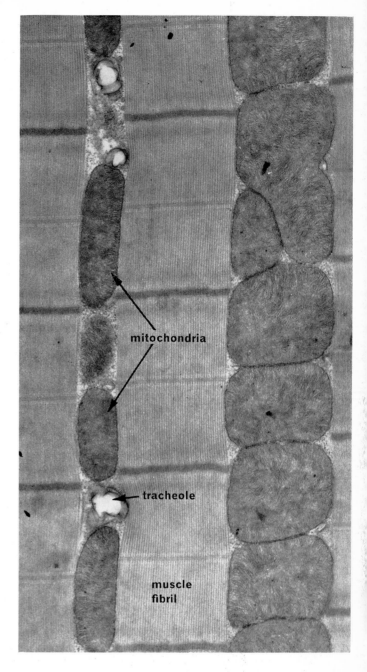

FIG. 6.6. Transverse section of flight muscle of *Pieris*. The mitochondria in insect flight muscle are branched structures which partially surround bundles of muscle filaments. *Magnification × 24,000.*

From Smith, D. S., in Rev. Canad. Biol., *Vol. 21, 1962*

FIG. 6.7. Longitudinal section of flight muscle of *Polistes*. The mitochondria are regularly arranged between fibrils of muscle and are opposite the 'A' bands in many cases.

From Smith, D. S., in Rev. Canad. Biol., *Vol. 21, 1962*

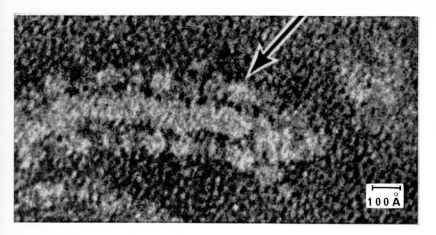

FIG. 6.8.   Part of a crista is shown here. To its surface
are attached granules (arrowed) of about 80 Å diameter. These granules are thought to be the sites of
the respiratory enzymes of the mitochondrion.

Photograph by H. Fernandez-Moran,
in A Textbook of Histology

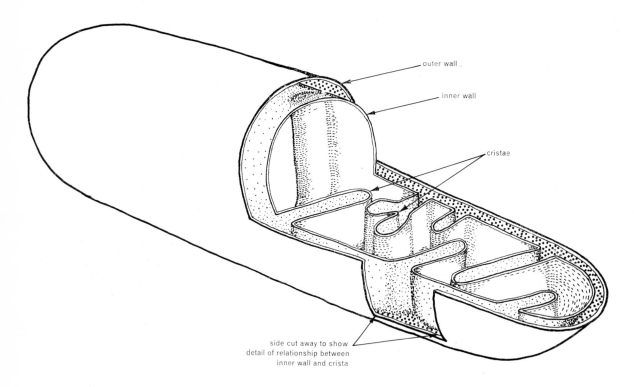

outer wall

inner wall

cristae

side cut away to show
detail of relationship between
inner wall and crista

FIG. 6.9.   Stereogram of a single generalised mitochondrion to show the relationships of inner and outer
membranes and the cristae.

7 · The Centriole

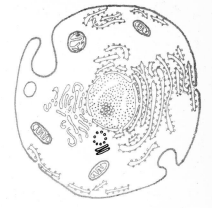

Every animal cell appears to contain a pair of centrioles, usually located in the hyaloplasm but near the nuclear envelope. The members of the pair of centrioles are often orientated at right angles to one another (Fig. 7.1). Each consists of nine paired filaments arranged in a hollow cylinder about 2000–3000 Å long and 1200–1500 Å diameter (Fig. 7.2). Two rings of rounded bodies, the satellites, each 700 Å diameter, connected to the outer surface of earth centriole by bridges, have been described (Fig. 7.3). These are not found regularly and may be transient structures. The centrioles separate at cell division, forming the centres from which aster fibres radiate (Fig. 7.4). The basal granules of cilia are derived from the centrioles. In spermatozoa the filaments of the tail are in contact with one centriole. In the retinal photoreceptor cells the filaments of the connecting cilium appear to originate from a centriole (see Figs. 10.1 and 10.2).

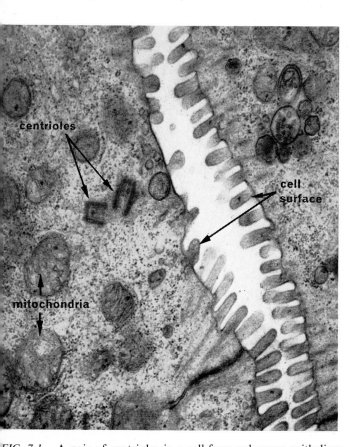

FIG. 7.1. A pair of centrioles in a cell from columnar epithelium of chick duodenum.

Photograph by S. P. Sorokin, in A Textbook of Histology

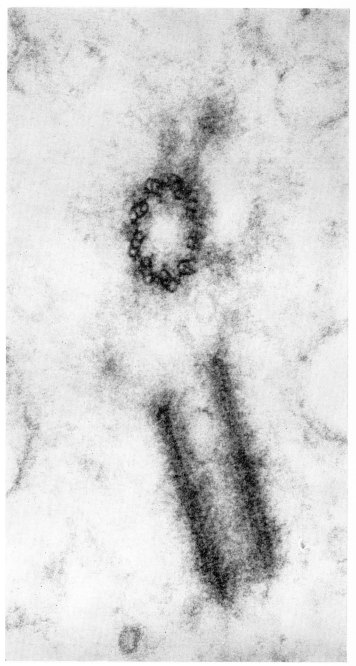

FIG. 7.2. Centrioles from human lymphosarcoma. The centriole structure is very similar to that of a cilium as seen in cross section (cf. Fig. 9.1). *Magnification ×155,000.*

Courtesy of Dr W. Bernhard

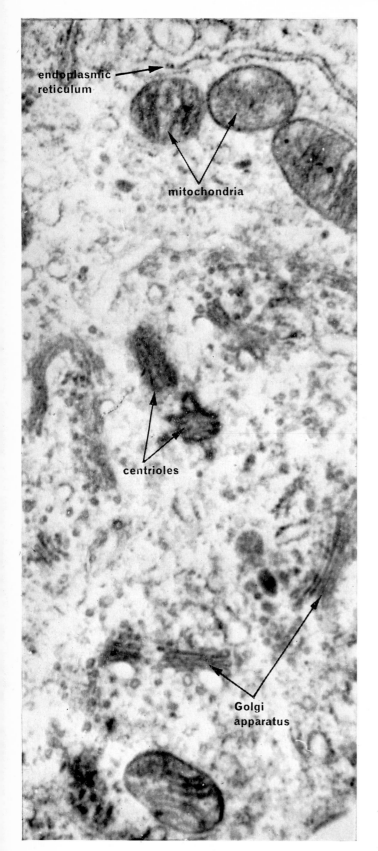

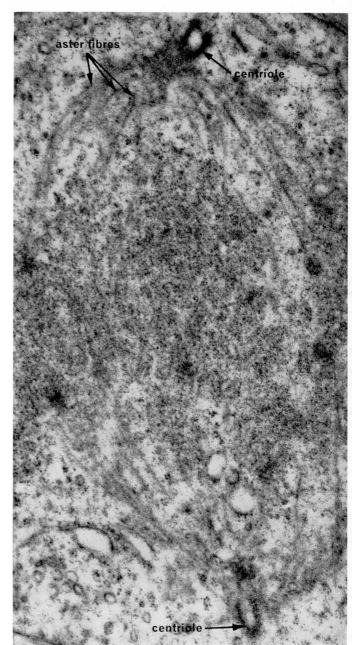

FIG. 7.4 (*above*).   Centriole with aster fibres from a dividing cell.
Magnification × 27,000.

From Bernhard, W. and De Harven, E., Fourth
Int. Conf. Electron Microscopy

FIG. 7.3 (*left*).   The centrioles are lying surrounded by the membranes of the Golgi apparatus. Satellites can be seen on the
lowermost centriole.

From Bessis, M., Ultrastructure of Cells, *Sandoz Ltd, 1962*

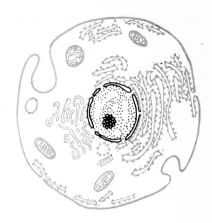

8 · The Nucleus

Typically every cell of an organism contains a highly specialised region—a nucleus. The size and shape of nuclei vary widely from species to species, and also from tissue to tissue in the same organism. For instance, nuclei of human polymorph leucocytes are irregular in shape, while liver cell nuclei are spherical. There is also notable variation in the chemical com-position of nuclei, for although all nuclei are alike in that they contain deoxyribonucleic acid, the quantity of which is constant within the nuclei of organisms of any one species, its composi-tion varies widely from species to species.

The nucleus is only partially separated from the cytoplasm which surrounds it by the nuclear envelope (Fig. 8.1).

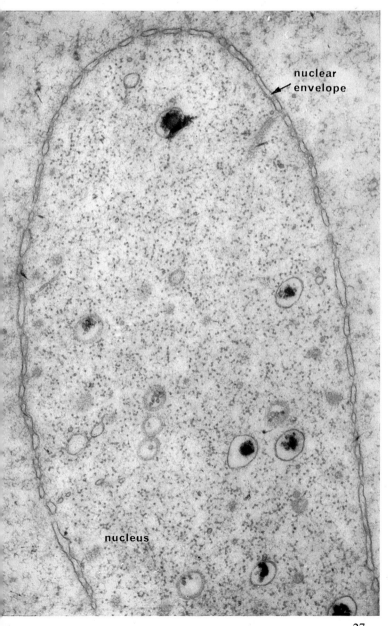

nuclear envelope

nucleus

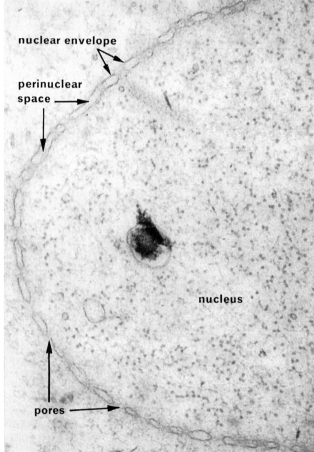

nuclear envelope

perinuclear space

nucleus

pores

FIG. 8.2 (*above*). From oocyte nucleus at a higher mag-nification. The perinuclear space and the pores in the envelope can be seen. *Magnification ×63,000.*

From Lanzavecchia, G., in Fifth Int. Conf. Electron Microscopy

FIG. 8.1 (*left*). Nuclear envelope in frog oocyte. Pores in the nuclear envelope are clearly seen. *Magnification ×40,000.*

From Lanzavecchia, G., in Fifth Int. Conf. Electron Microscopy

An understanding of the nature of the envelope around nuclei is of great importance in any theory attempting to explain how the coded nuclear information influences the physical and chemical activities of the cytoplasm. Photographs of the nuclear envelope show it to be a double membrane (Figs. 8.1 and 8.2). Each membrane is similar in structure to the other cell membranes. The outer membrane is granulated like the rough membrane of the endoplasmic reticulum but the inner membrane is smooth. Both membranes are each about 50 Å thick and are separated by a space of 200–400 Å, called the perinuclear space (Fig. 8.2). Pores of 400–1000 Å diameter have been demonstrated in the nuclear envelope many times (Fig. 8.3). It is not known for certain if the pores are open permanently or only from time to time. Some cytologists claim to have evidence of the passage of substances through these pores from the nucleoplasm to the cytoplasm. As there is structural similarity and morphological continuity between the nuclear membranes and the membranes of the endoplasmic reticulum it has now become recognised that both are probably part of a single membrane system (Fig. 8.4).

During cell division the membranes of the nuclear envelope break up into small fragments. Part of the envelope around the daughter nuclei re-forms from fragments lying in the cytoplasm. It has been suggested, but it is not certain, that these fragments are those formed by the breakdown of the parental nucleus, but there must also be some system for synthesis of new membrane.

During the interphase between successive divisions, nuclei can usually be seen to contain one or more nucleoli and a ground substance that often appears to be structureless or to contain a chromatin network.

The chromosomes, which become visible only during cell division, are thought to be distributed in the chromatin network during interphase. The nucleolus does not seem to be an organelle for it is not surrounded by a membrane. Chemically the nucleolus is rich in ribonucleic acid which is different from the rest of the nuclear RNA and which is thought to be derived from the chromosomes. The RNA accumulates at a particular place, the nucleolar-organising element.

There is one of these on a single chromosome of each haploid set of chromosomes, and here the substances are organised into the nucleolus. Little structure is to be seen in electron micrographs of the nucleolus.

At the present time electron microscope techniques have been unable to add much information to our knowledge of chromosome structure based on the detailed chemical and functional analyses of geneticists.

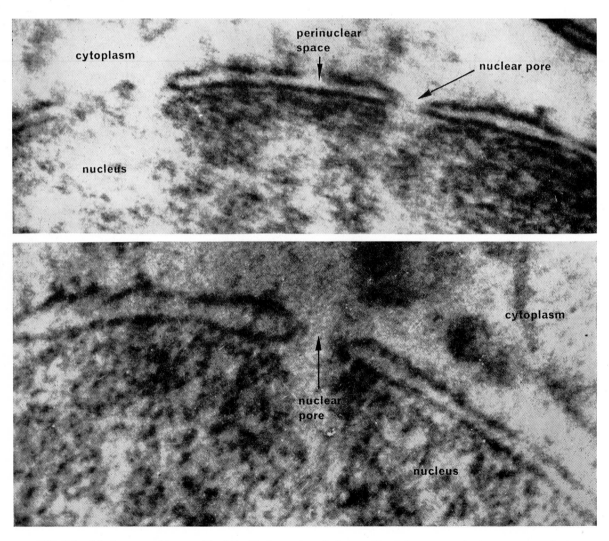

FIG. 8.3. Nuclear pores from acidophil cell of anterior pituitary cells of the mouse, shown at progressively higher magnifications: upper— × 199,000; lower— × 228,000.

From Barnes, B. and Davies, J. M., in J. Ultrastruct. Research, 3, 1959

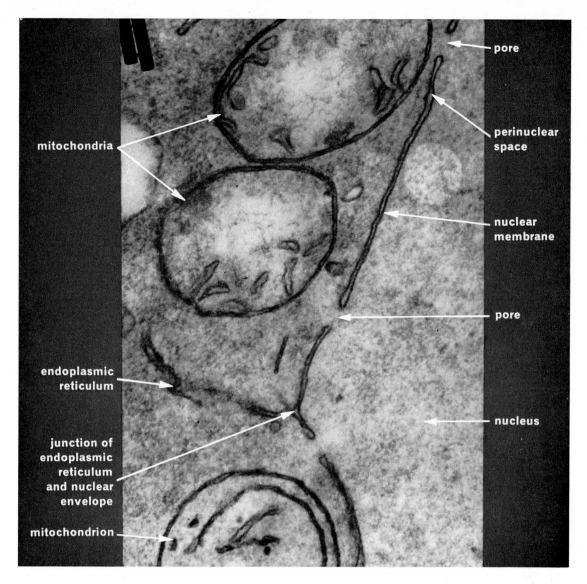

FIG. 8.4. Nuclear membrane from oxalis sps. The nuclear pores, perinuclear space and the continuity between the nuclear envelope and the endoplasmic reticulum are seen here. *Magnification* ×*15,000* (*approx.*)

From Marinos, M. G., in J. Ultrastruct. Research, *3, 1960*

9 · Cilia and Flagella

Cilia and flagella from all sources except bacteria seem to have a common pattern of organisation. Both are made up of fine longitudinal fibrils, enclosed in a membrane sheath which is continuous with the surface membrane of the cell. Flagella are up to 150μ long while cilia are shorter, often 5–10μ in length. Both are wider at the base than at the tip.

The basic structure of cilia and flagella appears to be constant. Inside the external membrane sheath there is an outer ring of nine paired fibrils surrounding a thinner pair of fibrils (about 200 Å diameter) which are enclosed in a central sheath. The outer paired thick filaments are oval in shape and about 180–220 Å by 300–350 Å diameter (Fig. 9.1). Both sets of fibrils grow out of the basal granule at the bottom of the cilium or flagellum; this basal granule is derived from a centriole. Viewed from the tip the outer fibrils can be seen to have a pair of flange-like extensions; these are not continuous along the length of the fibrils. The flagellum of Euglena and other flagellates, spermatozoids of the brown Algae and zoospores of some aquatic fungi have fine hair-like projections along their length.

There is at present no generally accepted theory of ciliary beat, conduction or co-ordination.

Cilia have been modified in several ways in the animal body. The cnidocil (which is the sensitive structure of the cnidoblasts of the coelenterates) and the rods and cones of the retina of molluscs, amphibia and mammals are modified cilia (see Figs. 10.1 and 10.2).

FIG. 9.1 (opposite). T. S. flagellum of *Trichonympha.* A series of flagellae in parallel flagellar grooves. In each flagellum the two sets of filaments can be seen very clearly. Around the central core there appear to be a set of nine very fine filaments. *Magnification × 130,000.*

Courtesy of Dr A. V. Grimstone

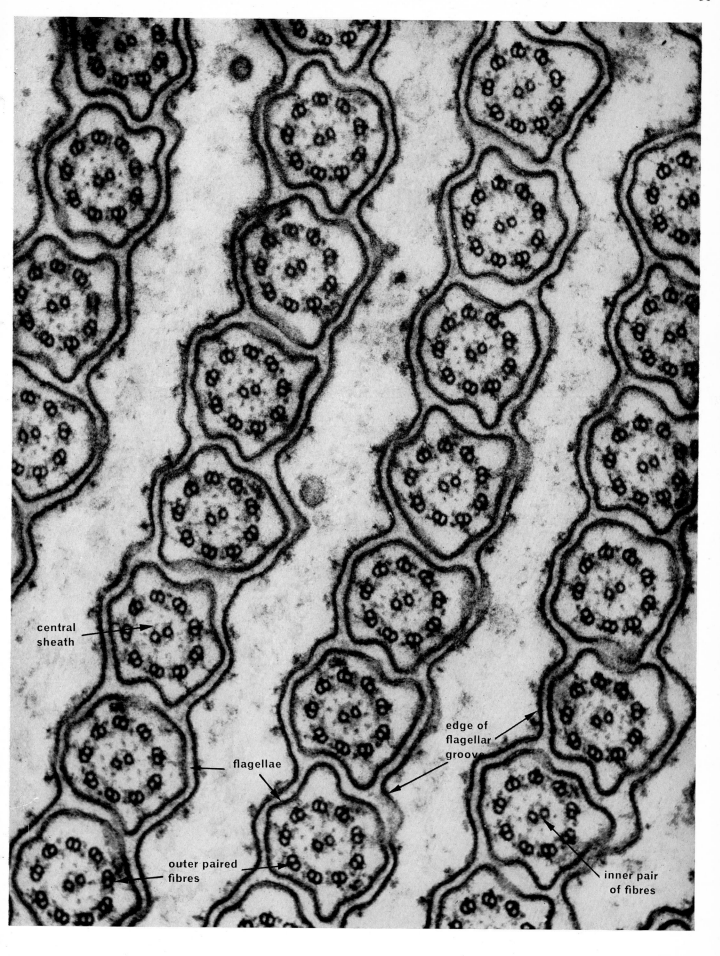

central
sheath

edge of
flagellar
groove

flagellae

outer paired
fibres

inner pair
of fibres

10 · Photoreceptor Cells

The photoreceptor cells of the retina, when stimulated by light falling on them, respond by initiating a nerve impulse. The photoreceptors (rod and cone cells) contain a visual pigment in which a photo-chemical change occurs when light is absorbed. It is this photo-chemical reaction which is the basis of translation of light energy into the electrical energy of the nerve impulse. It has been calculated that one quantum of light energy will bring about the photo-chemical change of one molecule of the visual pigment of the rod cell. It appears that as few as five quanta of light energy causing photo-chemical reactions in each of five separate rods simultaneously is the least stimulus perceptible in the human eye. Obviously the system cannot become more sensitive by any change in the rods themselves. Rhodopsin, the visual pigment in the rods, has been known since 1878 but the pigments of the cones have only recently been described, by Rushton in 1958, working with cones from the human retina.

In both rods and cones the pigments are located in the outer segment of the elongated photoreceptor cell. In both types of cell the outer segment, which is cylindrical in rods but conical in the cones, is filled with a stack of disc-like lamella arranged transversely to the long axis of the cell and enclosed by the plasma membrane of the cell. The outer segment of the rod is joined to the rest of the cell by a cilium-like structure called the connecting cilium (Figs. 10.1, 10.2 and 10.3). In transverse section, the connecting cilium can be seen to be made up of nine double filaments in a ring which are joined at their base to a typical centriole; a second centriole lies near the first (Figs. 10.1 and 10.2). The filaments run into the outer segment amongst the lamellae. On the basis of the anatomy of the connecting cilium, and as a result of observations made on retinal cells from very young animals, it is concluded that the outer segment is derived from, and is homologous with, a flagellum, and that the photoreceptors themselves are developed from flagellated cells that line the optic cup in the embryo. Cones in the toad have been shown to have a connecting cilium similar to the connecting cilium of the rod cells.

The lamellae in the outer segments of rods have been described as flattened sacs, which in the kitten develop from tubular invaginations of the plasma membrane, but in other animals from vesicles arising in the cytoplasm of the outer segment. Cone lamellae on the other hand seem to be made of single membranes (in the Perch) (Fig. 10.4).

In the frog these membrane lamellae have been seen to develop from infoldings of the surface membrane. The exact location of the visual pigments on the lamellae of the rods and cones is not known.

The remainder of the cell consists of a nuclear segment and an inner segment which may be contractile and sometimes con-tains coloured oil droplets. Both rods and cones terminate in a special synaptic region called the foot piece. The processes which occur between the breakdown of the visual pigments at one end of the cell and the transmission of a nerve impulse from the other are not known.

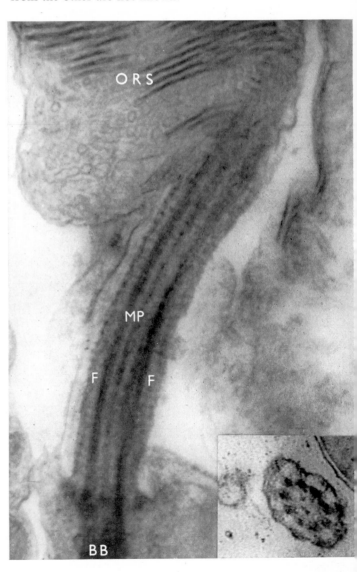

FIG. 10.1. Connecting cilium of mouse rod. The fibres (F) running from the centriole (BB) to the lamellae in the outer segment of the cell (ORS) are more clearly seen here than in Fig. 10.2. The inset shows the structure of the connecting cilium in transverse section—cf. Fig. 9.1. *Magnification* × 47,000.

From Causey, G., Electron Microscopy, E. and S. Livingstone, 1962

32

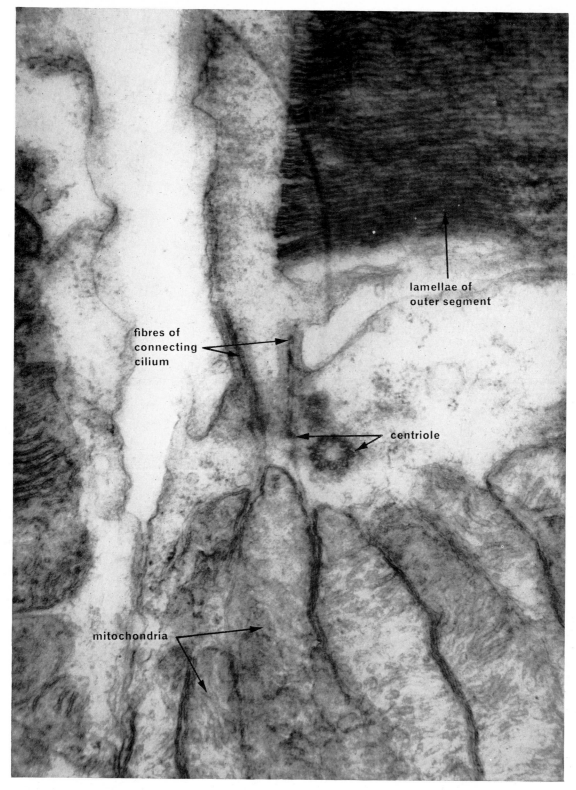

FIG. 10.2. Connecting cilium of frog rod. The centriole seen in transverse section shows the great resemblance to the cilium structure. The other centriole sectioned longitudinally provides fibres which run up into the outer segment of the cell. The upper end of the inner segment of the cell is packed with mitochondria in which the cristae are only indistinctly visible. *Magnification* × 75,000.

Photograph by E. Yamada (article by W. H. Miller), in The Cell

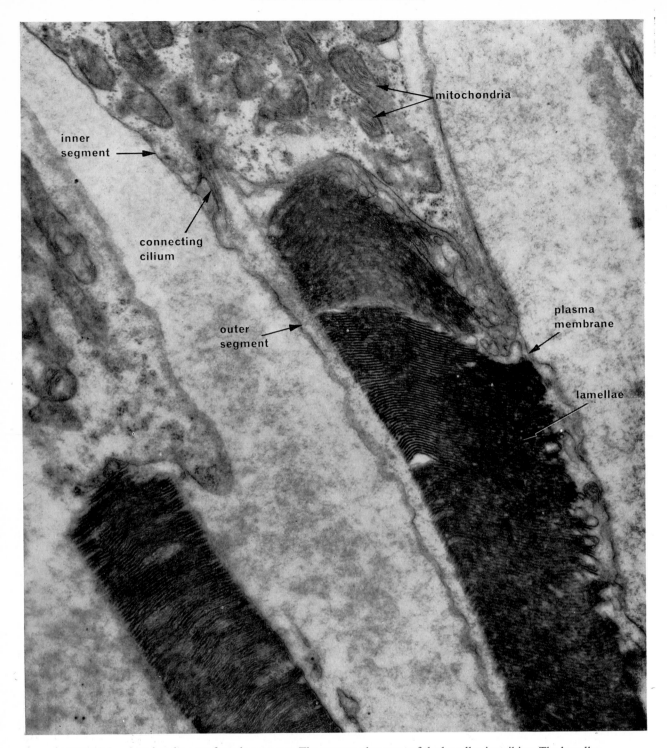

FIG. 10.3.   A rod and a cone from human eye. The very regular array of the lamellae is striking. The lamellae in the cone cell (on the right) can in many cases be seen to be double membranes. *Magnification ×28,000.*

Photograph by B. S. Fine (article by W. Rushton), in Sci. Amer., *207:5, Nov. 1962*

FIG. 10.4 (*opposite*).   Lamellae from outer segment of rod cell from frog retina. The two membranes which make up each lamellae can easily be seen. The fine granules (arrowed) may be artefacts but may be an indication of some structure on the surface of the lamellae.

Photograph by H. Fernandez-Moran in A Textbook of Histology

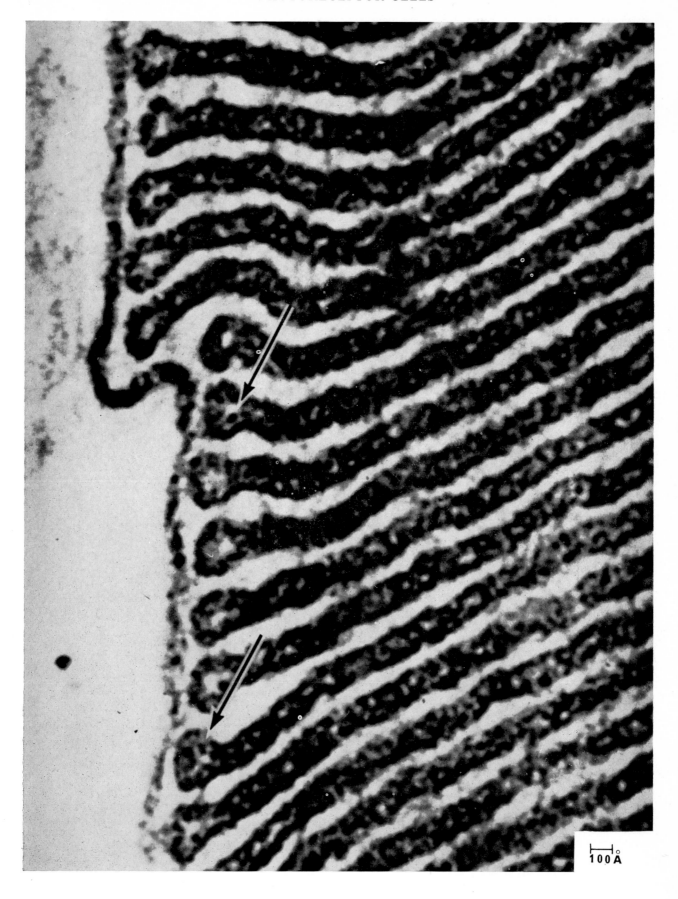

11 · Nerve Cells

The use of the electron microscope has increased our knowledge of the fine structures of nerve cells, in particular our knowledge of the myelin sheath. On the evidence accumulated by using conventional light microscope techniques it was suggested the nerve cells were of two distinct histological types: myelinated nerve fibres in which the axon of the nerve cell was covered by a sheath of fatty material called myelin (Figs. 11.1 and 11.3), and unmyelinated nerve fibres whose axons lacked a myelin sheath (Fig. 11.2). In both types of nerve cell the axon was considered to be covered by Schwann cells which formed a sleeve along the length of the axon and which lay outside the myelin sheath of the myelinated nerve cells.

Electron micrographs of unmyelinated nerve fibres show that while the axons are in close contact with the cell membrane of their ensheathing Schwann cells they are not completely enveloped by the Schwann cell. The axons appear to lie in grooves along the surface of the Schwann cells (Fig. 11.2). Immature myelinated nerve cells have a relationship with their Schwann cells which appears similar to that of the unmyelinated cells. But when mature the myelinated axon is surrounded by a tightly wrapped spiral of membranes (Fig. 11.3).

This spiral is continuous with, and is believed to be produced by and to be a part of, the cell membrane of the Schwann cell (Fig. 11.3). Just how the cell membrane takes up this spiral

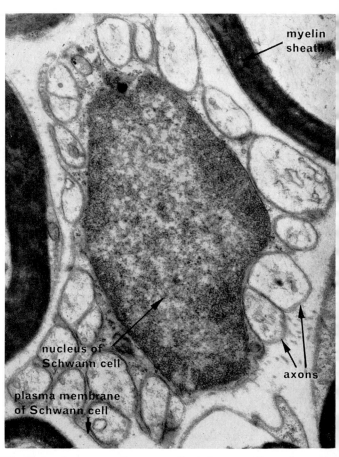

FIG. 11.1. A group of nerve fibres from the trigeminal ganglia of a 22-day-old rat. Most of the fibres have a thick myelin sheath, but small groups of non-myelinated fibres can be seen. *Magnification* × 5000 (approx.)

From Scott and Dixon, Anatomy for Students of Dentistry, *2nd edn. (E. and S. Livingstone Ltd)*

FIG. 11.2. A group of non-myelinated nerve fibres from the trigeminal ganglia of a 22-day-old rat. Each fibre is partially enclosed in Schwann cell cytoplasm. The nucleus of the Schwann cell is in the centre of the bundle of fibres. *Magnification* × 25,000 (approx.)

From Scott and Dixon, op. cit.

form is not known. It is, however, certain that it is the coating of membranes which corresponds to the myelin sheath of the earlier descriptions.

Periodically along the length of the axon the sheath is inter-rupted at the Nodes of Ranvier. Here the nerve cell is only covered by Schwann cells.

On this more recent evidence it appears that there is no fundamental distinction between myelinated and unmyelinated nerve cells.

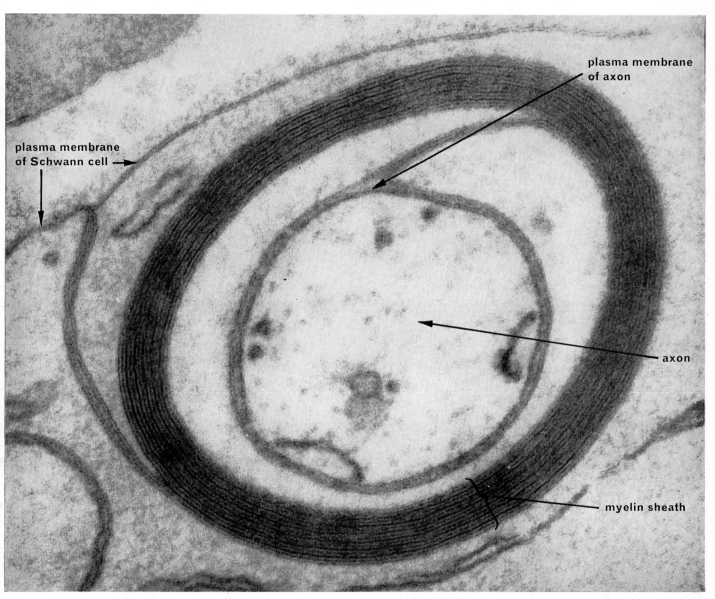

FIG. 11.3. T. S. sciatic nerve of mouse. The axon here is ensheathed in a much thicker myelin sheath than in Fig. 11.1. Exactly how the myelin sheath increases in thickness is not known. *Magnification × 180,000.*

From Robertson, J. D., Sci. Amer., 206:4, April 1962

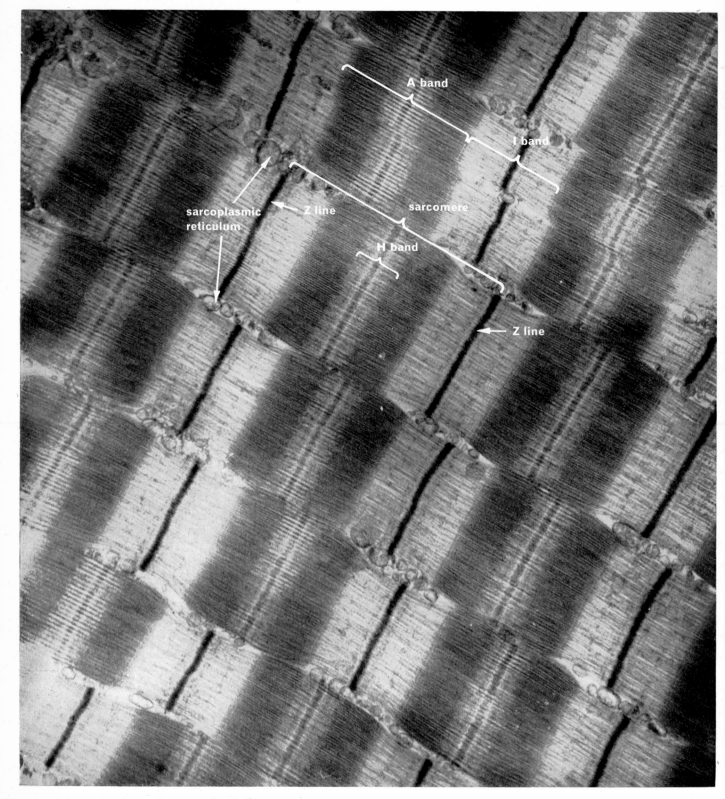

FIG. 12.1. Longitudinal section through psoas muscle of the rabbit. The sub-division of the cell into myofibrils and of the myofibrils into sarcomeres is very clearly seen. *Magnification × 36,000.*

Courtesy of Dr H. E. Huxley

12 · Muscle Cells

In vertebrate animals muscle cells are of two types: smooth (involuntary) muscles and striated (voluntary) muscles. Striated muscles also occur in invertebrates.

The striated muscles of vertebrates and anthropods are made up of cells 50–100μ in diameter, and up to several centimetres in length. Each cell has many nuclei on its surface. Beneath the cell membrane, which is called the sarcolemma, the cell is filled with long myofibrils, of the order of 1μ in diameter. There are also many mitochondria beneath the sarcolemma and between the myofibrils, and an extensive reticulum system, the sarcoplasmic reticulum. The myofibrils themselves are banded in a characteristic way. The bands are repeated along the whole length of the myofibril; the repeating unit of the pattern is known as a sarcomere (Fig. 12.1). Each sarcomere begins and ends at a band called the Z line. Between adjacent Z lines are two I bands and a central A band. The distance between one Z line and the next is the sarcomere length. This varies between about 2·0μ and 3·5μ according to the length of the whole muscle. The length of the A band within each sarcomere remains 1·5μ under normal working conditions of the muscle even when the whole muscle has contracted. It is these bands which, lining up across the whole muscle cell, give striated muscle its characteristic appearance (Fig. 12.1). In many muscles a regularly arranged transverse reticulum is seen throughout the cell; this is probably an invagination of the plasma membrane (Figs. 12.2 and 12.3). It may in some way keep the corresponding parts of the myofibrils lined up across the cell, and may also conduct the impulse which stimulates the muscle into the centre of the cell.

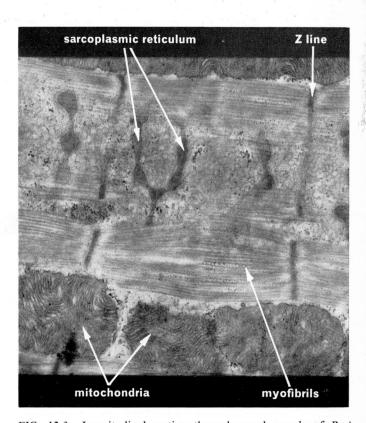

FIG. 12.2. Tangential section through coxal muscle of *Periplaneta*. Between the myofibrils many small tubes can be seen. These are the sarcoplasmic reticulum, here cut in transverse section. *Magnification* × 20,000.

From Smith, D. S., Rev. Canad. Biol., *Vol. 21, 1962*

FIG. 12.3. Longitudinal section through coxal muscle of *Periplaneta*. Three sarcomeres can be seen and across these run the branches of the sarcoplasmic reticulum. This section is taken at right angles to the plane of Fig. 12.2. *Magnification* × 20,000.

From Smith, D. S., Rev. Canad. Biol., *Vol. 21 1962*

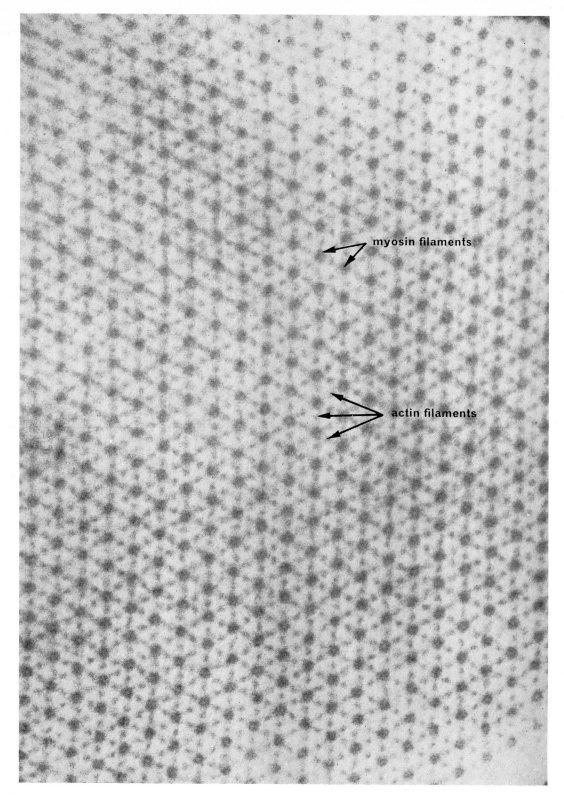

FIG. 12.4.   Transverse section of a fibril of flight muscle of aphid *Megoura*. Each thick myosin filament, about 160 Å diameter, has six thin actin filaments, diameter 90 Å, arranged around it, and each actin filament lies between a pair of myosin filaments. In mammalian striated muscle each actin filament lies symmetrically between three myosin filaments, but as in insect muscle each myosin filament has six actin filaments around it. *Magnification × 210,000.*

From Smith, D. S., Rev. Canad. Biol., Vol. 21, 1962

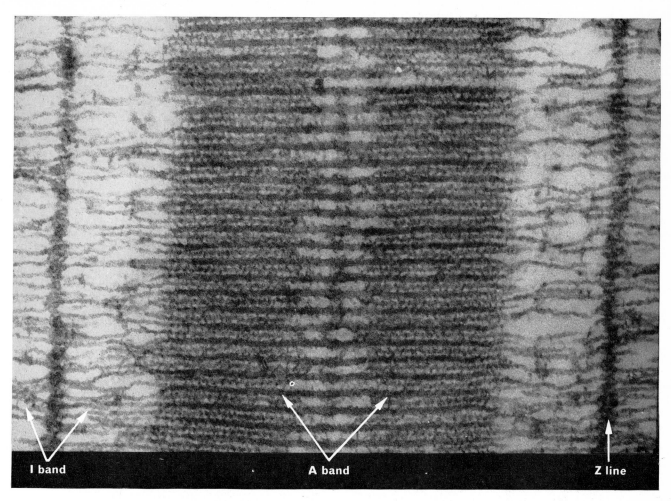

FIG. 12.5. Longitudinal section through a single sarcomere of rabbit psoas muscle. The subdivision of the sarcomere into *A* and *I* bands can be seen to be a consequence of the arrangement of the actin and myosin filaments in the sarcomere. The projections from the myosin filaments are very clearly seen. *Magnification × 122,000.*

From Huxley, H. E., in The Cell

At high magnification the *A* and *I* bands can be seen to be the consequence of the existence of two sorts of filaments. One type of filament about 200 Å in diameter and 1·5μ in length make up the *A* bands. These filaments lie parallel to each other and to the long axis of the cell and are arranged hexagonally; each filament is surrounded symmetrically by six others (Fig. 12.4). The *A* band filaments have helically arranged projections on their surface except at the centre of the *A* band. The other type of filament is thinner, about 70–80 Å diameter, and shorter, about 1μ. These thinner filaments extend from the *Z* lines towards the *A* band (Fig. 12.5). At a sarcomere length of about 3·5μ there is no overlap between the thick and the thin filaments, but at shorter sarcomere lengths the thin filaments slide into the lattice made up of the thick filaments

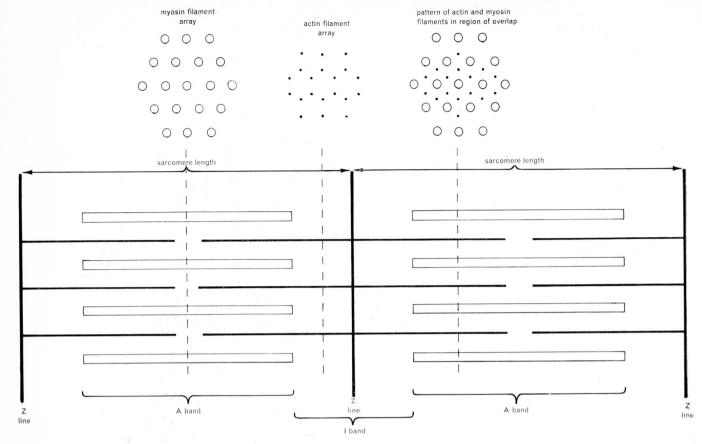

FIG. 12.6. Diagrammatic section through striated muscle from a mammal. The upper diagrams of transverse sections through three different regions of a sarcomere show the actin and myosin array. In the lower
diagram a longitudinal section through two sarcomeres at a relatively short sarcomere length is shown.

and their projections. At a sarcomere length of about 2μ the
ends of the thin filaments butt in the centre of the *A* band (Fig.
12.6). It is known that the thick filaments are principally made of
a protein myosin, and the thin filaments are principally a second
protein actin. The *Z* line is formed by actin filaments from adjacent sarcomeres branching and interweaving in a very complex
way. A protein, tropomyosin B, may be contained in this
branched structure.

The nature of the forces which cause the relative motion of
the two sets of filaments remains obscure.

Cardiac muscle is of the striated type, and differs from it only
in detail. The sarcolemma has deep invaginations which may
account for the branched appearance of cardiac muscle cells in
the light microscope and the opposing membranes of two cells

may correspond to 'the intercalated disc' of the light micro-
scopists. This disc may run in part across the myofibrillar
direction and in part parallel to it.

The cells of vertebrate smooth muscle are very long. They
are narrower than striated muscle cells only a few microns in
breadth. The cells are not split into myofibrils, but contain what
appears to be a single type of filament about 80 Å in diameter
(Fig. 12.7). There is no regular side-by-side packing of the
filaments of the kind seen in striated muscle. In addition to the
filaments dense bodies are also seen in smooth muscle cells.
Whether smooth muscle contracts like striated muscle by
relative motion of two sets of filaments is not known, although
proteins very similar to those from striated muscle have been
isolated from smooth muscle.

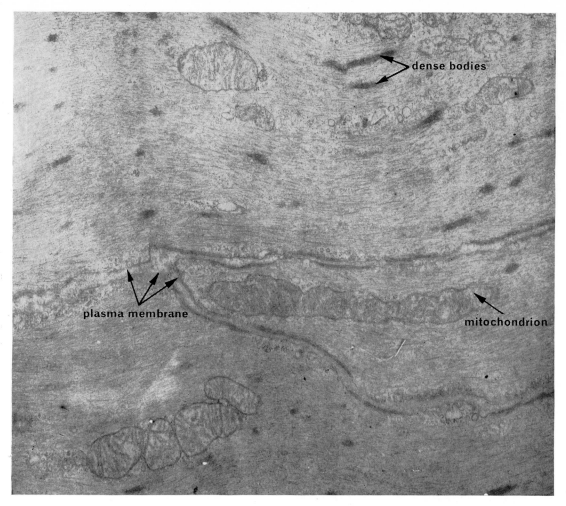

FIG. 12.7. Part of three cells from smooth muscle of chicken gizzard. Fine myofilaments can be seen and in each cell groups of mitochondria and scattered dense bodies. *Magnification × 15,000.*

Courtesy of Dr K. Schoenburg

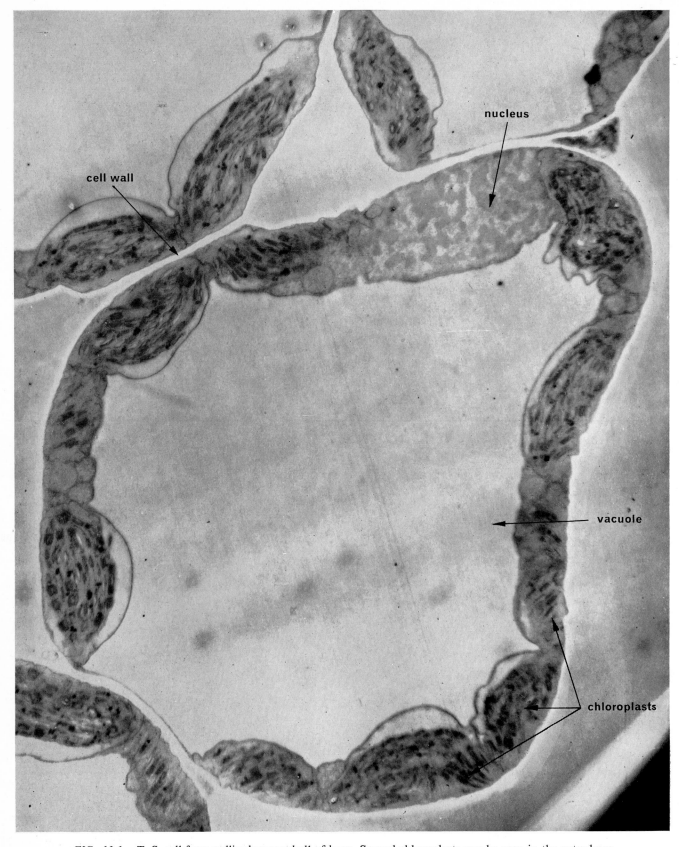

FIG. 13.1. T. S. cell from pallisade mesophyll of bean. Several chloroplasts can be seen in the cytoplasm of the cell. The centre of each cell is taken up by a large vacuole. *Magnification ×5800.*

Courtesy of Mr A. D. Greenwood

13 · The Chloroplast

In the cells of all plants in which it occurs, except in those of blue-green algae and bacteria, the green pigment chlorophyll is contained entirely within the organelles called chloroplasts (Fig. 13.1). These are the sites at which photosynthesis, the conversion of radiant energy into chemical energy which may be stored within large molecules, occurs. Chlorophyll plays a central role in this process for it absorbs radiant energy and so initiates photosynthesis.

Chloroplasts are of various shapes and sizes, but those of higher plants are often shaped like a biconvex lens about 4–6μ in diameter and 2–3μ thick. The number of chloroplasts in a cell varies from tissue to tissue, from plant to plant, and during the life history of a single cell. Juvenile cells commonly lack chloroplasts but contain numbers of submicroscopic bodies, the proplastids, from which choroplasts develop as the cell matures.

Mature chloroplasts in the higher plants are very complex. The basic unit of their structure resembles a flattened hollow tube-like structure the walls of which are single-unit membranes. The flattened tubes, or chloroplast lamellae, are enclosed by a double-walled chloroplast envelope and embedded in a protein-containing fluid called the stroma. The chloroplast lamellae are differentiated into two regions: the grana and the intergrana regions. In sections cut along the length of the chloroplast the lamellae appear to be parallel to the long axis of the chloroplast for much of their length (Figs. 13.2, 13.3 and 13.4). At various points a group of adjacent lamellae make contact with each other to form a neatly layered stack. In surface view the areas of contact have a circular outline; with the light microscope this is seen as a dark green point called a granum. In early electron micrographs of dried fragments of chloroplasts partially disintegrated grana were observed and likened to piles of discs (Figs. 13.6 and 13.7). But the chloroplast lamellae making up the granum continue into the region between grana. Here, however, they are not in close contact with each other. This region is the intergranum region (Figs. 13.3, 13.4 and 13.5).

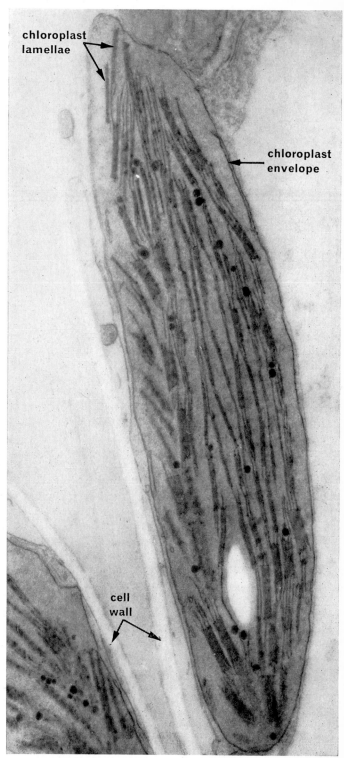

FIG. 13.2. L. S. single chloroplast from mesophyll cell of bean. The outer chloroplast membrane is double and surrounds a complex system of flattened hollow tube-like lamellae. *Magnification ×32,000.*

Courtesy of Mr A. D. Greenwood

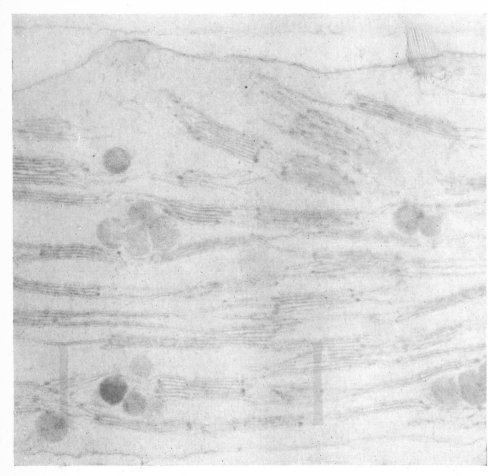

FIG. 13.3. L. S. chloroplast from mesophyll of bean. The lamellae make contact with other lamellae along part of their length. These orderly stacks are the grana. But the lamellae are continuous from one granum to the next.

Courtesy of Mr A. D. Greenwood

The stroma lies between the lamellae in the intergranum region but is absent from the grana. The lamellae in the intergranum region may branch and join up with other lamellae, and each lamella may pass through several grana (Fig. 13.4). The exact details of the system have not yet been worked out.

The structure of the chloroplast evidently varies from one plant species to another. For example, in spinach there are between 40–60 grana/chloroplast, each granum 6000 Å in diameter and 800 Å thick, but in tobacco there are 40–80 grana/chloroplast. The number of lamellae per granum also varies from 20–30 to 100 per granum in Aspidistra, and from 10 to 15 per granum in tobacco.

Biochemically the chloroplast is highly organised. Chlorophyll is certainly present on the lamellae in their grana regions and may be present in their intergrana regions as well. The lamellae isolated from the other chloroplast components have been shown to be able to liberate oxygen from solutions when illuminated, but present evidence indicates that they do not fix carbon dioxide. On the other hand, the watery stroma contains enzymes essential for the fixation of carbon dioxide. The stroma also contains granules which, although smaller than ribosomes, resemble them in two ways: they contain RNA and they take part in protein synthesis. Starch grains and fatty globules frequently occur in the stroma. The starch appears to be a product of photosynthesis. The role and origin of the fatty globules are not known.

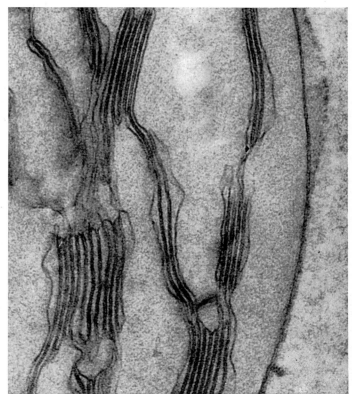

FIG. 13.4. L. S. chloroplast from bean mesophyll showing lamellae in several grana and the intergrana areas. They appear to branch and rejoin particularly at the edges of the grana. *Magnification × 80,000.*

Courtesy of Mr A. D. Greenwood

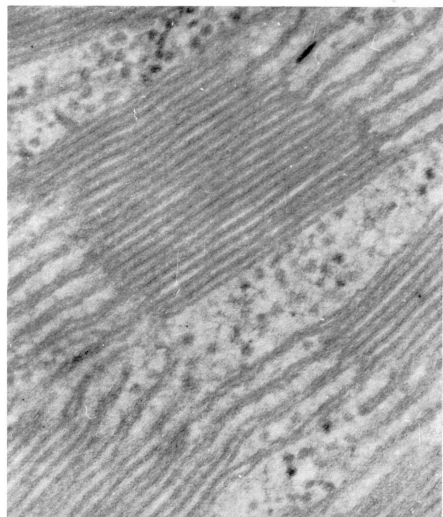

FIG. 13.5. The relationship between the grana and the intergrana areas can be very clearly seen here. Large and small granules can be seen in the matrix material. *Magnification × 180,000.*

Photograph by A. E. Vatter (article by A. L. Lehninger), in Sci. Amer., *Sep. 1961*

FIG. 13.6. The grana in this plate have been squashed sideways, appearing like a pile of discs. The intergrana lamellae are not visible using this technique.

From H. Leyon, Exp. Cell Res., *7, 1954*

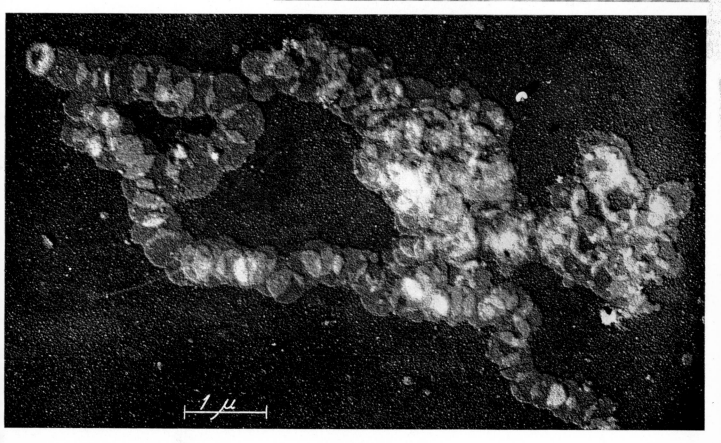

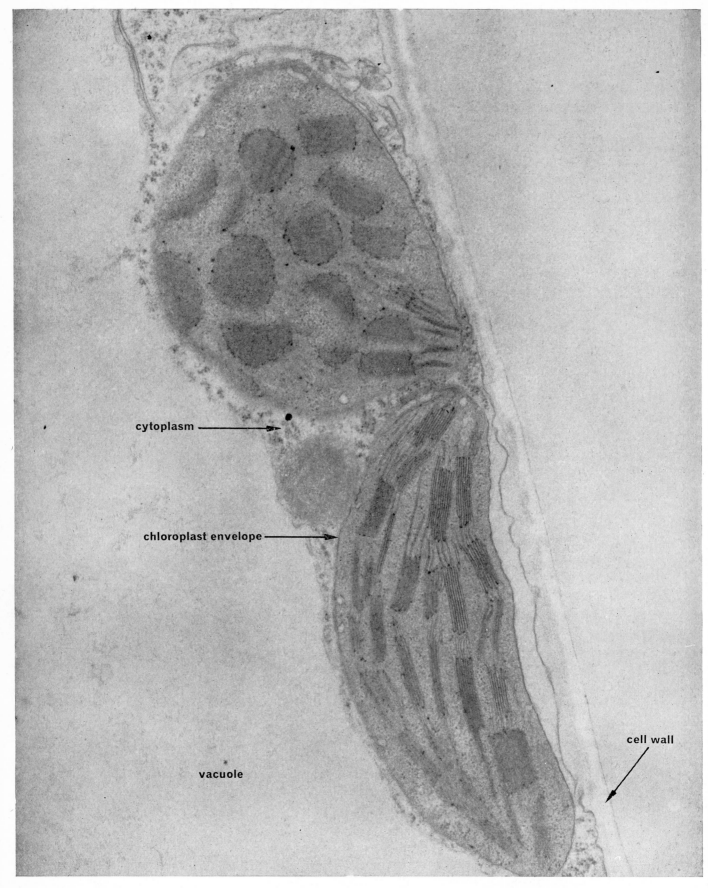

cytoplasm

chloroplast envelope

cell wall

vacuole

FIG. 13.7.   Two chloroplasts are shown, one in which the lamellae run along the length of the chloroplast, and in the other grana are seen in surface view as circular patches. *Magnification ×22,600.*

Courtesy of Dr B. Gunning